This book belongs to:

In the beginning,
there was nothing.
Only emptiness
and darkness...